Frame of Mind

poetry
by
Timothy B. Anderson

also by the author:
Poser: a sketchbook of ideas for artists and models

All Rights Reserved
Published by Cygnet Press

ISBN: 978-0-9833-4982-2
LCCN: 2011903472

For Larry

Table of Contents

Love and romance...

All that remains...

House of cards...

Love and romance...

Carnival in Red

A romantic Latin rhythm vibrates
and soulfully sways deep into the night
caressing and teasing artful dodgers
moving in unison on the crowded floor.

The moonlight and the madness
hauntingly tugged at my obsessed being
as the throbbing bass drove and twisted
in perfect tempo with pulsing drums.

Keyboards and quarter notes tickled in tune
with swirling dresses and soaring feet
while stars twinkled and electrified each partner
with unbridled and equally untamed passion.

An amorous sax segued toward the dawn
sultry and sensuous in its urgency
to unify and propel the consumed assemblage
into a state of euphoria and divine release.

A woman in red undulated others aside
as she was stricken by the harmonies lilting
from deep within each executioner of the muse
as they became one and one became all.

Wishful Thinking

I am touched . . . and directed
to turn left instead of right.
I cannot see the author
of the suggestion
and I do not know
the quality of the message.
But I turn anyway and go
away from known comfort
and stability into the flow
of the new direction
that offers no promises.
The hallway of my mind is dark
and narrows in the distance
with only a pin-point of light
to lead me along its path
of implied safety.
There are no fears to bind
my flight of purpose
to the next level of
who I am in the eyes of self.

Ghost Writer

and so i write
to let you know
what's going on
and to tell you
how i feel today
sometimes sense is made
and then—not
and so i write...

Ode: for Anna K.

On a mountain of stone you weave your magic
to and through the basket's ageless reeds
with hands gentle and a heart full
of love that has been faultlessly given
unselfishly to and from—all.

Like a pack-rat—I carry you with me
tuck you under a well-worn pillow
or into a corner of a silent night's dream
where I see your scribbles—clear
in images and words and I remember.

The hearth is made a little warmer
and the house a little bit fuller
holding you within my heart-of-hearts
blinded by the whimsy of your charms
and enlivened by the comfort of your arms.
As an embryo is carried into a waiting world
I have been bearing your grace in time
to a rhythm and dance waiting in line
as others have fallen to and fro
preying on lust and fantasies alike.

It is of no matter or consequence
whether it is today or the next
but the time will indeed come to pass
when mere distance cannot separate
a bond ignorantly strengthened by time's advance.

An Ethereal Blessing

With nothing between us but the night
and the warm gentle glow of the candle's light
we rode on the magic carpet of an ocean wave
and watched the stars come out to play.

The whisper of the wind tickled my ear
and dried my eyes when I shed a tear
for you are all I have ever wanted or needed
to make my life at last full and complete.

The patterns and the fabric of our lives
have been woven with care and insight
as we attempt to sort the confusion in our hearts
while urgings of the Others demand we never part.

My being is awakened and passion is inflamed
for we are wild animals that cannot be tamed
as Cupid and Eros beckon from the other side
to remind us that a spark ignited is hard to hide.

My heart is willing to follow the lead . . .
taken in trust in order to fill the need
of hands held out in order to touch
a part of another that's needed so much.

So I have composed for you this little rhyme
that may lead you to a place in time
where your spirit is free and willing to learn
all that it can with no bridges to burn.

It is written from a place deep within my soul
that is never young and can never grow old
and within a dream I have seen many times
for it is all part of love's eternal paradigm.

Apparitions...

All that remains...
are the shadows of your smile
around each and every corner
as I needfully race toward
your memory—teasing.

All that remains...
is the veiled and graying mist
of a love that has faded
and is obvious in its absence
and oblivious to my pain.

All that remains...
is the always empty side of the bed
where we showed we cared and dared
to explore our souls deep into the night
when we shared desires and dreams.

All that remains...
where my saddened heart once was
is an empty space alone and blue
torn apart and missing your touch
and searching for reasons why you had to go.

All that remains...
is me—without you.

Mary in the Mirror of Time

Your primal beauty was first shared by angled twigs
covered and dripping with colored earthen clay
and driven by the ignorance and desire of a lover
uncertain of what his eyes had beheld.

Kingdoms and lives were lost and won
as Kings and Princes as well as Gods alike
fought to possess what they couldn't hold
when you seductively winked and walked away.

Many a feather has wavered as it moved from
an almost empty ink-well to a page of parchment
as a stricken poet sought to capture the moment
when his heart felt your presence for the first lasting time.

Duels have been fought in defense of your honor
and blood has been continually spilled
while gunfighters and writers died for your love
without a chance for your hand or your bed.

And now there is me—with a trace of you
already penetrating my unarmed softened being
captured and captivated by the magnificence
of your passional influence in the awakening of my life.

I am guided by the compassion of your blue eyes
and the warmth of your heart and soul
as a guide-dog might lead a blind master
through the maze of a sightless life of lost love.

Mystical masks and statues revealed throughout eternity
bear the reflection of the contours of your timeless face
as well as the fullness of lips and the curve of hips
that continue to conspire and inspire sword and pen.

Page by effortless page as my life unfolds into you
I am both thankful but also regretful of the time I have lost
winding around corridors without end or guiding lights
on my way to me and the discovery of the essence of thee.

Caught

We stole a kiss
Or two
You and I
We stole a kiss
That wasn't a lie
We were caught
In an embrace
That neither guilt
Nor time can replace
What will they say
Who will they tell
Are we guilty
Of being caught
In love's jail
We stole a kiss
Or two
You and I
We stole a kiss
That wasn't a lie

Safe and Sound

So she sleeps
slumbering
safe and sound
unaware of tomorrow
but hopeful.
A program of love
expected
plays ignorantly
within the confines
of her mind.
Warm thoughts
of urges fulfilled
after a day
of draining demands.
How do I tell her
goodbye . . .
as she sleeps
slumbering
safe and sound
unaware of tomorrow?

For Each Other

My pen urges me to write...
without command
as the nectar of our love
flows majestically from
this dime-store utensil
which seems like a sabre
sent by the Gods to issue
a Decree of Divinity
upon your unsuspecting soul.

Word upon romantic word
then line by caring line—continues
as if the source of this magic
is an endless and lazy river
fed by the liqueur of our ecstasy
and upon which many a poet has trod
in vain efforts to expound on the
beauty of their ignorantly intended-to-be.

Centuries of fanciful sonnets
arrive on the pages of my passion
as if they were obsessed tributaries
flowing from the minds of lovers
descendant from countless ages past
while your sighs dry my tears
as your fingers relax my senses
while your love warms my expectant heart
and we know—we are here for each other.

Rising and Falling

Rising and falling,
a chest once more filled
with the luxurious air and beautiful scents
of the French house on 10 rue Ferlus.
A vision in the dappled sunlight
and slight shadow of the second floor window
where I worked and wrote
in that Soreze summer as a breeze played
with the hem of her dress,
gently teasing it up and down.

Nipples harden beneath the thin cotton garment;
perhaps from a dream of pleasure,
a dream of love among the clouds
as her body shifted, ever so slightly;
breath quickening, chest rising and falling,
a mouth barely open as if to release
the build up of heat and passion while
hands moved lazily across her stomach
with one moving slowly to a breast
the other slipping to a place...below.

The clip-clop of shoes and sandals
served to announce people
walking along the narrow street below,
seeming as music to her ears,
while she continued the play begun
with the draw of the curtain
and the opening of the window...
I was careful to not move too quickly, too harshly,
during this afternoon of slow movements
and undisturbed luxury on pillows and quilts.

Good-bye... Hello

In a span of time scarcely known
we began with a mighty roar
with mutual satisfaction superbly realized
on levels few will ever achieve
when my heart was opened wide—again
as my soul quaked in obvious joy
with visions of long-awaited completion
and realization of endless prayers answered.

Honesty and truth of the highest order
were virtues espoused by you and I
as we spoke of concepts and ideals
which were readily agreed upon
as I spoke of love unequalled—to share
willingly given to all in your life
while I emptied my pen in valid tribute
to the rainbows you brought into my world.

But clouds of fear and doubt...
began to erode and undermine the magic
of what was and could have been
as you began to withdraw in retreat
then too soon the voices of the same wind
started to separate and confuse
issues that were greater in scope
than a mortal unity ignorantly denied.

The closer we compulsively grew
the more invisible you became
while endearing terms widened the gap
to a distance too soon beyond measure
and choices of ease were made in confusion
to relieve unknown fears which lay deep
as we released and said . . . goodbye.
before the time was taken to say—hello.

Departure

as i walk along the beach
and the cool white sand
leisurely sifts
through my toes
i think of you
and how beautiful
and wonderful you were
the night before you left
then i start counting
the seconds
til you return
****

your voice was warm
as it flowed through the lines
i was glad to hear its softness
you said you just called
to say "Hi."
are you sure
or was it just an alibi?
******

as the days go by
and i think
of spending the future
with you
the past
is easier to forget
******

pieces of love
cast with the wind
along sun-swept beaches
washed away by waves
once here—now gone
forgotten...

In Time

And does he whisper
sweet somethings in you ear
while he tells you
how very much he cares?

When you come home
as the work-day is done
does he warmly remind you
that you still remain—the one?

But how can you tell
if his pledged love is real
when to be satisfied
you have to beg borrow or steal?

You've given your all
and taken it to the limit
you know—the time is now
you can't waste another minute!

New horizons have been opened
to be joyfully experienced
as there are no more locks
it is time to scale the fences.

There is a fresh day dawning bright
as your fated path becomes clear
and the choice has rightfully been made
in time for the coming of a New Year.

Morning Rain

She stands there—by the paned window
as cascading rivulets of rain
run the course of their uncharted journey
in complete and beautiful silence
on the other side of the window.

Inside—the patrons remain in awe...
of the lingering lyrical magic
rendered as her sensitive fingers
caressed each element of the instrument
of her passion with assertive precision.

Haunting melodies and whimsical tunes
filled each corner of the receptive chamber
while she performed a symphony of love
on that gray and drizzled day...
and—I will never be the same.

Note after sensuous note took us
on a fairy-tale ride to majestic mountains
sunlit endless beaches of white
and vibrant valleys of brilliant green;
as she played intimate tag with—the morning rain.

Just to Be

I like looking at you
as you sit across from me
with your hair flowing
and your body melting
into the grassy sea.
As a leaf floats effortlessly
and silently lands
upon your up-turned knee
your eyes lazily open
and you playfully wink at me.
Many times I have come here
just to be near
the beauty of your face
and the calm of your smile.
Just to be.
Just to be.
While the sun radiantly shines
and a sportive breeze
tugs at the branches
of a nearby tree
I close my eyes
and I wonder if
it could ever be
You and me.
You and me.
It's now getting late
as evening's clouds roll in
while I look across the way
I notice you getting up.
Then I wonder if
I will ever see you again.
Just to be.
You and me.

Remembering Dreams

She felt an unaccustomed trembling a quaking
from a place that only her heart
knew the direction to ... or from
as it lay dormant and still waiting.

He was different than she remembered
flowers were brought for no reason
and he kissed her in broad daylight—in town
and went for rides in the subtle moonlight.

"He must be mad," they told her
as they chided behind the strength of his back
and away from the love in his voice
when he began to welcome all into his arms.

A warmth returned to her porcelain cheeks
fallow and ashen from an eternity of passion's neglect
for their life-giving blood had been let
into a river of complacent regularity.

A new rhythm embraced their lives
as they made time for themselves and each other
in lives that had been diametrically opposed
following paths laid before by consciousness in confusion.

And on that warm summer afternoon by the pond
when she understood the words for the first time
flowing delicious from ancient parchment to pen
her satisfied heart remained open and—waiting.

Thoughts...

passion flames
heightened by your touch
or the mere whisper
of your voice...
building and bellowing
in ignorant silence
arrested for trespassing
into a moated heart
which is in glorious receipt
of your billowing emotions

***

Clouds
white and fluffy.
Sky—
bright and blue.
You—
warm and loving.
Clouds—
stormy and gray.
Sky—
dark and rainy.
You
good-bye and gone.

I Wait

And so I wait
for the telephone to ring
so I can ask you superfluous questions
that have no answers.

And so I wait
to find a note from you
in my mailbox with superfluous questions
that have no answers.

And so I wait
to tell you I love you
and that I can't get you out of my mind
or keep you away from my heart.

And so I wait
for you to tell me you love me
and that you can't get me out of your mind
or keep me away from your heart.

And so I wait.. and I wait.

Ode: Toulouse Lautrec (after *La Toilette*)

"Only once," you said. "I will pose for you,
 only once, and no one must know.
I will tie my hair in a *chignon*, and
I will turn my back to you,
with my face lowered, away from prying eyes.

"You will not see me without a dress,
or from the front to expose my treasures;
the chemise will be lowered to my waist,
and a spread will cover the floor, under my
stockings I will not toss over the chair.

"You will paint my hair the color
of fire, and straighten the curls
to keep prying eyes and minds away
from the face, the chin… me.

"You will paint me here, where I sit,
in my toilette, but a different
scene will be painted,
one in which your studio
is forefront and foremost." she insisted.

I would have painted her anywhere,
be it farm or factory, studio or salon;
for her beauty was beyond compare,
her hair silky and soft, falling in cascades
past a shoulder the color of porcelain.

Only that once have I posed her,
but I have painted her a thousand times
with each stroke of the brush,
each curve of the crayon,
and with each movement of my hand.

Universal Guidance

The forest and the flowers
and the birds and the bees
paid silent homage in tribute
to the extended display of love shared
and retroactive passion spent
on the timeworn carpet of green
that spread out under them.

The lovers had entered nature's house
saying little—but thinking aloud
on this warm and beautiful summer day
as thoughts of shared lifetimes to come
complete with all that was desired
were becoming patient and rewarding realities
away from prying eyes and vengeful souls.

Soon their affection would be unveiled
no longer having to be hidden and unspoken
as the integrity of their mutual bond
carries them through meaningless days
and seemingly endless lonely nights
with a vision of roses and moon-beams
replacing forgotten pledges and lost hope.

Through a void of constant confusion
destiny has beckoned them with a muted song
to rightfully acknowledge that which is theirs
in all its magnificent and wondrous glory
while paired hearts become full—at last
and conscious minds open to the universe
to recognize the voice which has steadily guided them.

Secrets

as the moth
nears the flame
and the fly
nears the web
as i—in turn
fall in love
with you
******

does our love show
it shouldn't
does anyone know
they couldn't
when can we tell
we wouldn't
******

we laughed
we snuggled
we loved
each other
******

when they saw me
in the morning
after loving you
they wanted to know
why I was smiling so
******

the game we play
is a farce i say
we work all day
and love the night away
and nobody knows
or do they...

Snapshot

I lay in my bed tonight
with only a snapshot of you
to make love to.
As I oblige willingly
and allow your soft blue eyes
to undress me...
your arms are remembered
as they wound their way
through the rumpled sheets
still unmade form the last time
to my waiting soul.
Now when I close my eyes
I see your skin—glistening still;
a lucid reminder of mutual satisfaction.
I miss you and I love you
while a snapshot is a lesser remembrance
it's all I have... for now.

The Rain and You

A reflection of you
is how I think of the rain
as it cascades from the sky
whether in endless torrents
or gentle silk-like layers.

The incredible magnitude of storms
remind me of our love
as it unfolds without restraint
whenever we are together.
Then a steadily increasing downpour
is likened to the momentum
of our wondrous relationship
as it grows—day-by-day.
The hypnotic effect of a rainbow
compares to the feelings experienced
when I explore the sensual contours
of your shamelessly willing body.

The rain and you...
together—as an example
of the epitome of nature
in its most inspiring form.

Adagio for Francesca

and a tear fell...
to the expanse of a naked breast
from a quivering chin
streaming unheeded and around
a breast,
bare and full of the lust and love
that was theirs
in that summer of her yesterday
between the Camels and Buds
and the sacred Formica
that welcomed virgin brandy
while Nature lay in witness
of a time too soon in the passing
but etched in the memory
and a tear fell...

Muse Me This

How can you
not
be my muse
when every
day
you guide me
with love
and compassion;
with lust
and desire
to fulfill
my every
wish,
my every
fantasy?

Naked Prisoner

And there she remained
after...she stood before him
naked to his soul
and imprisoned by his gaze.

From the edge of the darkness
she brought a ray of light, of hope
into his life of confusion and apathy;
an existence of absolute mediocrity.

She promised nothing, but gave
so much more than was asked
by this stranger to her life;
this person of the past.

Digging ever deeper into his being
she prodded, picked the truth out
strand by tenacious strand, until
nothing was left but his nakedness.

He had cried out in the wilderness
but had never gained response
to his desire and passion, until
he was all but spent and bent.

A Tangle of Sheets

An afternoon's delight
on a borrowed bed
flowed deliciously
between fresh sheets
without effort,
with only a trace
of youthful fear
to guide you and I
to a place never
forgotten
in heart and soul.

With little more
effort
than it took
to slide you
out of
a flowered summer dress,
your shoes,
panties & more;
and me out of
jeans and cotton shirt,
we rode
a collective wave
of passion & lust
with only the hush
of the wind
as witness.

A Presence of Heart and Soul

As an apparition, an ethereal, ghostly presence
you have remained in my life
and forever reserved a place in my heart
for you to reside in wait.

A vision of peace is something I remember
as I see you walking away, back toward me
with your face directed to the future
and to the life that had been chosen.

Throughout the years the ties have remained
stronger in absence than in attendance
but forever and prominent in my soul
as I awaited, in silence, the return of your smile.

But years disappeared without thought
and no communication was pursued
finding life and love apart from each other
we dutifully worked out the kinks of self.

Trickling into the vessel of conclusion
lives and loves have come and gone
into and out of one and the other
but still, the ties remained in ignorance.

Split-aparts we became, once found, never lost
into worlds of our own choosing
but perhaps not of our destiny
as we now stand in wonder of it all.

If I Had Known You

If I had known you...
before my journey began
I could've danced with joy
without the agony of the pain.

If I had known you...
I may have seen brighter days
and at a much earlier age
I might have learned how to play.

If I had known you...
Stress would have been less
and people would've known me
with little anger—and more happiness.

But, if I had known you then
I wouldn't be who I am today
with un-learned lessons still to come
and I wouldn't have known to stay.

If I had known you then...
I might not have learned to love
sharing may still be unknown
and I wouldn't have trusted the spirits above.

But, I know you—now
as I feel you in my heart
and all I had to do
was wish on a falling star.

Mirrors of My Mind

The mirrors of my mind...
have kept you close to my heart
no matter the distance separated
we have never been apart.

The mirrors of my mind...
have known you would return
to the place we left so long ago
with more lessons to be learned.

The mirrors of my mind...
have known how hard it would be
to believe in what has happened
and understand the power of destiny.

The mirrors of my mind...
have allowed the way to be clear
and the doors to remain open
for the return of a friend, so dear.

The mirrors of my mind...
have continued to stand in awe
of the wonder of the future
and the blessings of it all.

Holding Still

I sit here holding still.
Waiting is not unknown to me.
This year began with a quiet resignation.
How this year will end eludes me.

Rather I will not allow myself
The illusion of the unknown.
I want the delicious sense of spontaneity.
I want to open like a water lily.

The knowledge of our union
Is a mystery of creation.
I do have memories of your soft lips.
I have an ocean of magic in your words.

Musings #1

On the eve of our tomorrow
my heart leaps with anticipation
while my soul seeks solace
in the knowledge of our union.

Less than yesterday...
but almost too many to bear
the days languidly slither by
as my senses become heightened.

On the eve of our tomorrow
I attempt to console myself
with single snapshots and poeticisms
that come from your heart of hearts.

But I know you are near
and that serves to comfort me
in the twilight of my nights
while I wander to corridors of my future.

On the eve of our tomorrow
the end will justify the miles
we have traveled in the quest
for who we have become.

Musings #2

Forward into the void
we go without a net
to catch us if we fall.

Into the midst of the many
remain the few who choose
to go to the edge of the dark.

From the dusk comes the dawn
of a new day that leads us to
the spring of our lives.

Going from one end of yesterday
and forging on the path of tomorrow
we will join in the present.

Musings #3

Ah, but the wait
more than we want
but less than yesterday
and soon to be over.
Thirty-five years compressed
into but one moment
waiting for the touch
eager for the sight.

Tonight you join
me in slumber
and walk with me
in the solitude of my dreams.

So, goodnight....
lady of my nights
and think of me
as you wrap yourself in slumber.

Soundings

I stood in the darkened doorway of her bedroom
amazed at her beauty and peacefulness
while she lay, tangled in wrinkled sheets
across the room, unaware of my presence.

For more than thirty years, I wondered
what became of the girl I left behind
on that warm, apprehensive day
in the borrowed apartment and bed.

For many years I reached out across the universe
without response until a wayward
missive served to awaken my interest
and kindle my unrequited pursuit.

In porcelain perfection the girl became a woman
as I touched her, again, for the first time
and my fingers traced a familiar pattern
along a rising breast to a hardened nipple.

Beside me, now, she is resting in peace
content from a night of pleasure
as a warm ray of sunlight caresses her curves
and bathes her in a sea of tranquility.

She smiles herself awake and turns toward me
with open arms as I succumb to her desire
and relax into her newly familiar, seductive spell
as it carries me into submission.

Forever is as long as I would have waited
for soft, passive perusings along her spine
while accepting the union of our bodies
on the morning of our charted, destined future.

Traveller

In exploration of...
the sinewy corridors of his life
tentacles controlled direction
while ignorant purpose served
to draw him away from
a patient heart in the waiting.

In exploration of...
the cacophonic canyons of his soul
he laid in wait for expectant completion
of a mission yet to be determined
on the way to the charted destiny of
a patient heart in the waiting.

In exploration of...
the pebbled highways of his heart
a man continued to cast his line
into turbulent waters of dubious lucidity
as metaphoric truths drew him to
a patient heart in the waiting.

Backroads....

The alleys have narrowed
and passage is trying
but I persevere with hope
guided by a light
that shines from afar
beckoning me to come
toward the peace offered
a weary soul on the mend
and a heart in the waiting.

For centuries too long forgotten
man and woman have danced
to the sweetened music of Pan
who plays a tempting tune
for two into one lovers
who sway to a melodic rhythm
of subtle pleasure and passion
ignited by the charred embers
of a fire too long in the making.

Tomorrow is but another day
for the two hearts in search
of completion and compassion
on the way to a future already written
and yesteryears too long gone
as mysteries of the mind
continue to confuse and contort
feelings on the rise
and souls in search of redemption.

Simple Me This

What could be more simple
Than love between the two
Who care about nothing else
And vow to cherish none other
Than the one who holds
The key to it all?

What could be more simple
Than holding a timid hand
When crossing a street
Or pulling the one closer
To the other bursting with the love
That will keep them fully alive?

What could be more simple
Than looking into the eye
And seeing the beautiful reflection
Of the one who has been waiting
Through the years and through the tears
That fell in want of an unfound love?

What could be more simple
Than finding the you who never was
Until the circle at last became complete
When a call was ignorantly answered
And cast into the void of a timeless need
Seeded by the absence of connection
And sown by the presence of fruition?

Simple me this . . .

The Key

Line after line of timid communication
Opened the dialog of our conversation
While knowing little of each other
And even less of ourselves
We progressed past the point
Transgressed by many
On the way to holding the key
To a door long shut but seldom locked

Just on the other side of tomorrow
Our hopes possibly linger in wait
For a future unknown in the past
And a marriage of the minds goes forth
With no beginning or end in sight
As one step is taken after the other
On the way to holding the key
To a heart and soul in the waiting

But there are no obstacles or walls
To block our progression to the passion
That can only be the result
Of the inevitable union of the fusion
To be enjoyed by the two who
Choose to live life with eyes wide open
On the way to holding the key
To a path of glory and gratification

And still we talk in riddles and soliloquys
With words between the meanings
That separate and hold at bay
Emotions left in check and sheltered
By years of solitude alone and without
The one who seeks to be sought
On the way to holding the key
To a puzzle written on wings of flight and fancy.

Alone...

in a world of misconception
ignorance and silent witness
we tread into a space
reserved for only those
who choose to live
a life unfettered by guilt
recrimination or greed

Alone...
in a world of choice
we tread, ever so boldly
into a space devoid
of fear or envy
and we reach out
to the other who waits
for the other who waits

Heart Poems

In the solitude of my dreams
I cannot quite see your face.
I have waited so long it seems
that I wonder if your presence
is a creation of my fantasy.

Are these words on the page real?
Or are they illusions of hope?
Whenever I stumble, you reassure.
When I become untethered,
You pull me back.

I can't quite fathom your heart poems.
They go to a depth unknown to me.
They awaken a place thus far untouched.
In the solitude of my dreams,
I remember your blue eyes.

The night is cold and clear.
The sky a deep shade of indigo blue.
The stars shine their light from a distance
as far from me as you it seems.
It is you I want to be near.

Interruption

As the day opens
and a warm sun
finds its way
through a barely
cracked wondow
I think of you

While I am driving
from one place
to the other
and to nowhere
in particular
I think of you

When I am writing
a poetic rambling
or a subtly suggestive missive
and I search catacombs for
the key to divine inspiration
I think of you

When I am called for sleep
and I have kept
too much of the day inside
away from the source
of its cacaphonic din
I think of you

And when I am dreaming
of a soft, white winged creature
tempting me to follow
its wingspread to a place
known by only a few
I think of you, only you.

One..... for you.

All is well
but I miss you
as a mother misses her child
as a cloud misses the sun
as the rain misses the thunder
as the sky misses the ground
as an Eagle misses its young
But I miss you, and, yet
All is well.

Another one...... for you.

A part of life
is all that poetry is
as it greets you
with the sunrise
and walks you through
the beauty of the day
while whispers of grace
glide into your speech
and the wind gently
lifts you as you walk
and tucks you in
as you sleep
and that's all poetry is
Just another part of your life.

All that remains...

Coming Home...

Seeking webbed desires
on the other side of tomorrow
into the veiled arms of the past
a love runs away from self.

The passion that resides
in his heart of hearts
knows that the truth is hidden
between lines of accepted reality.

In an attempt to mask
approaching familial fears
of uncertainty and ignorance
a love retreats into the shadows.

Unknowing to those in or out
and continuing to run into the fog
he listened to the words of wisdom
spoken in his soul of souls.

He is coming home...
as a tear falls on his childhood
denounced of its hold and strength
and—a love begins life anew.

Equilibrium

Gaps, slices of freedom
dot the day and fill the night
of my life, one that strives
for absolution of self-inflicted
liability. But the octopus stretches
tentacles farther than escape
from the turmoil,
the possibility of capture
can be fancied.

As Hercules fought
to gain the balance
of the globe, I seek
the equalize a yen-yang
existence, out of grasp,
out of synch; But the
surface is slick-smooth and
difficult to gain a foot,
any semblance of stability.

Were it not for tendons
and muscles and ligaments,
and ligaments and bones,
the fabric that makes the quilt of life,
I would plummet into a
milky bog, harmless to most,
insignificant to some,
forgotten by the rest
as no tributes will sound
my passing; none will wave me
gone; a kiss me
off, perhaps, but no...

I am a trifle, at best,
not even a pair to the hand;
four cards to draw
and not a match!
A meager existence
carved out of blood-and
sliced, piece by piece until there
is no more juice, no more feeling;
lifeblood seeping, soaking,
letting itself
be carried on the wind, porous
to the touch, invisible to the eye.
I will go and I will be gone.
And it will be done, at last.
A soul was touched, a hand offered,
but no response...no response.

Solace of the Soul

Sitting in this room, on this foreign soil,
I seek to claim some of which was lost
along the way the to man I have become,
in the hope of gaining solace and peace
of mind and of soul, and release of grief.

There are places I cannot go and houses
I cannot enter without a proper key
for the entry into halls of discovery
and cellars of doubt and despair;
guilty without trial, sentence conferred.

Many are the soliliquys to render freedom,
soulless phrases to ponder in the silence
of the visitation of the symphonies of pain
with little in the pleasure of the task;
tripping over debris strewn by seekers past.

At the window of this centuries-old stone house
I look out over the valley and picture the years
spread long into the distance and picture
a past of plenty, complete without loss;
another fairy tale of no means… no matter.

As the day ends, the future will be what it will be,
and the hope of discovery begins with the shards
that have sought to cloud fulfillment of a soul
hungry for the solitary mending to begin
as doors remain ajar, needless of locks and keys.

Infinite Journey

Windswept images sprinkled along a stretch
mile after mile upon timeless beaches
sandy or rocky but always here or there
to remind us of our brittle mortality
as we seek to understand the infinite mystery.

Destiny is a deep hole—black as a moonless night
extending anonymously from beginning to end
inviting entrance without promise of an exit
but offering hope in the place of failure
and doors to nowhere and everywhere without a key.

Urgings of destiny whisper your given name
lingering seductively on each syllable
with hypnotic gestures signaling your soul
through corridors of confusion to the conclusion
of what has been written on eternal pages of stone.

Step by step and day by day we travel in time
looking for the other that some never find
while we hope for union and comprehension of reason
for living apart from and beyond each other
until the final piece of the puzzle signals the end.

Unison of spirit driven by ignorant desire
carries us onward and outward toward other planes
devoid of the fears we harbor beneath our masks of life
awaiting wondrous recognition and sublime release
so that we may be all that we wish and know we can be.

Parable for a Poet

And what of these words I write
that have incubated since birth
who knows of their value
or the breadth of their worth?

The muse that moves me
urges me on day after day
and will it ever happen
that I have nothing to say?

Inspiration that comes from within
has more meaning when let out
but in order to make sense of it
sometimes I have to shout.

Those who choose to listen
have ears that are open wide
and believe in the clarity of truth
without the deception hiding in lies.

Words seeming to appear between lines
sometimes have no rhyme or reason
and no longer can I hide them inside
no matter the time or the season.

As I continue to flow into form
there is little thought of what will be written
or what will make the cut into significance
of a life left for the learning of the discipline.

Passages: for JJ

We can only hope that if there is no response to our prayers
or appeals—or our aspirations become diminished and faint
that in spite of it all we are doing the correct deed
and we are following our divinely-directed course.

With the gentle rain comes the clouds that demand
to be recognized as they persist in dampening our
spirit while extinguishing the lingering embers
as only ashes linger and the weight of a thousand
fears; both known and unknown continue to plague
our daily decisions with innuendoes of suppressed doubt
and deepened wounds of unqualified guilt.

But as the drizzle trickles from the sky so too
does it serve to cleanse and from behind the
fog of confusion we can emerge victorious in our
patience. Then as the sun shyly peeks from beneath
the cover of nature's camouflage we are reminded
of silver linings and unseen signals which remain hidden
to those who refuse to see for want of ignorant expectancies.

Now, with lucid vision we can be calmly led to that
place which had remained in reserve yet finally realized.
As with the added wisdom of our experiences we can begin
to understand the value of our presence and the effect
we have on those we love and those we do not appreciate.
In the unfolding comes the receiving; and in the letting go
comes the giving—knowing that we have done all we can.

Whether our desires become memories or truths we can be
re-assured that whatever path is laid before us it will be one
of enlightenment and discovery; which can only lead
us to believe that we are moving in the direction... for us.

Release

Try as we might
We cannot separate the past
From the future
But, then, who is to say
Whether or not it matters
That shards of our yesterdays
Permeate the shadows of our future
And enable us to cross
A tenuous bridge without a net
As friends and family alike
Shake heads in less-than-subtle disbelief...

Knowing the bond is from the heart
Enables you and I the take the chance
On a future riddled with uncertainty
But filled with lucid vision
Of all that it could be
For those who choose
To chance swim the river
Instead of...
Clinging to the sandy shore
Of security and empty acknowledgement
With only a lifetime to fulfill...

Soaring

After months of attempting to fly
The young Sparrow became dejected;
Saddened by his apparent failure
Until he almost gave it up for good.
But on one fateful and defining day
He thought he would give it one last try
Because he really knew he could fly!

Climbing to the longest branch
Of the tallest tree in the forest
He looked down on family and friends alike
Who were booing and hissing at the trembling bird.

But their jeers only served to strengthen him
And give him even more cause for success
As he fluttered his tiny wings and tip-toed
All the way to the tip of the highest branch.

With his beak held high
And the gift of a strong wind
He closed his eyes and spread his wings
And jumped into the air, unafraid.

At first he sputtered and turned
And began to fall toward the earth
Then as if by magic he began to turn
Upward, ever upward toward the sky.

Finally mastering his flight
He flew toward those gathered below
With mouths held open and eyes bulged
Standing in witness to a miracle.

The brother and friend they had known
Had disappeared and was no more
For what they saw was not the flight of a Sparrow
But the soaring of a grand and glorious Eagle.

Where Is My Hero?

Where is my hero—who left when I was one
and took my dreams before my journey had begun?
With no one beside me as a mentor along the way
many wrong turns were made as I went from day to day.

Where is my hero—to guide me through my teens
and teach me how life isn't always what it seems?
From adolescence to puberty I hardly knew what to do
and there was no one to tell me that life had many hues.

Where is my hero—as I seek to learn the truth
is he gone forever like the forgotten days of youth?
Whose voice do I listen to as each day is done
and who can I ask to finish the myth never begun?

Where is my hero—as I gently take her hand
to tell of the birds and bees and warm feelings so grand?
To speak of rites of passage and turning a boy into a man
while whispering about the power of love and making a stand.

Where is my hero—as we exchange our wedding rings
to remind me of my duties and other silly things?
He is in my past and it tugs at my mind...
while I have been told that some things are best left—behind.

Where is my hero—to remind me of what I've learned and seen
is he tucked away forever behind my childhood screen?
How will I face tomorrow if I can't learn from my past
and if I forget everything...how long will I last?

Where is my hero—to help me greet another wonderful day
while giving me assurance that he is with me even when I play.
I am sure that he stands beside me—whether I see him or not
to offer guidance as I journey toward my own...Camelot.

Rattle Bones

An idyllic island existence that lasted
more than 10 years,
two children and 17 jobs, ended
with a shaky signature on paper
as I made my way to Seattle in 1982,
to heal pulsing wounds of indifference and betrayal
that created an ocean of silence; lasting
longer than necessary between
the mother of my children and me.

It was a new lifestyle
more designated by circumstance
than design;
as I struggled through timeless days
and seemingly endless nights
to find the way
to where I thought I should be
in the hooded eyes of self.

An omen, that of something
to be taken against its will
wrenched me awake
from a wary and fitful sleep
on the first night
of my first weekend in Belltown,
in a second floor, Murphey-bed studio.

Urgency cautiously beckoned me
toward the barred window,
half open against a windy,
foggy and wet night,
as I leaned forward, in the kitchen,

on the Formica and chrome table
for balance and saw the heavy chain
on my cycle,
a thin barrier for a thief,
stretched almost past the point,
as senses became stirred
and the somber scene
readied me for what was to come.

In the early afternoon of the next day
a gun sounded,
begging collective attention,
where across the street
from the Avenue Restaurant,
a greasy spoon of ill repute,
a body rested, stagnant,
on the street, blood pooling
the length of a shoulder
as nothing moved.
No response. No repeats. No life.

Arms branched out,
like parents reaching
to catch a falling infant,
to slow me in my effort
to lash out, to shout at the guilty.

"Don't. You'll be next. They don't care,"
I heard, in chorus.

Still, I wanted to do something,
to help the dying.
But the voices echoed in my soul,
rebounded in my mind,
resonated in my heart.

Turning my back,
with my neck craned to the scene,
I began to walk,
cautiously, to my new home, a place...
rich with danger,
rich with life,
rich with death.

A block away, everything
was still slow-motion silent,
but for the sound of the uniformed blue boys
yodeling orders to you and me;
canons on deaf ears.

A block away, everything
was still slow-motion silent,
but for the sound of the uniformed blue boys
yodeling orders to you and me;
canons on deaf ears,
acoustic rhapsodies without melody or pace,
staccato urgings of obeyance and order.
"Just another vagrant caught holding the bag,"
said one badge to the other.

But the man with his face
melting into the pavement with a heart
that would beat no more—had
a briefcase, not a bag;
a career, not a handout;
a family, not the street;
a life, not a death.

"A young cop," a man in blue said.
"Made an honest mistake."

Death captured the day,
like a crowd in awe of the passing
of the Pope,
and stilled the night
while we were witness to rites of passage
for the badge and the bullet.

Along the littered avenues
and on soiled concrete benches
beds were made,
again, that night,
of newspaper and prayer to still the demons
and summon the Angels for a night of
requiem and repent among the steel drum fires
and—brown bag drunks.

In the ghostly alleys of the box dwellers
the cast of the (nightly) First Avenue Follies
pursued unrecognizable dreams and nightmares
as they clapped
trembling, rickety hands,
stomped angry, calloused feet,
praised to Him on high,
and feverishly—rattled them bones.

Flickers

Graying morning at
the Ballard Bridge,
encrusted, weathered railing
welcomed me to my final stand,
the final arrow at Little Big Horn,
and an early reveille
as concrete walls
extended themselves
for passing cars, slowing
in ignorant witness
of blood chilled
to icy tributaries;
dulled mind flickering
a lifetime of images,
hopeless memories-and
phantom feelings.

Flowing turbulent in time
with a river, 100 feet and
two or three heartbeats below,
rocks for severing and water
for sucking, and
standing at a crossroad
allowing one leg to
absent-mindedly, but
with lemming-like exactness
pursue the other
to the spot, the last flight
from supposed critical pain;
headlights flash,
headlights flash:
green, yellow,
red,
        red,
                red!

Phoenix Rising

Even though the road is unpaved
and filled with pot-holes,
covered with debris and branches;
with sharp angles to disrupt my journey,

yes, even though the road is unclear
and only the faintest of lights shine
to light the way; still I go,

like a lemming on the edge of a precipice,
still I venture into the darkness
of my spirit where I know
I must reside until

the blanks are filled-and
holes in my life are none,
and there are no more
questions without answers;

no more birds left in the nest
to wonder what to do with their lives,
how far to spread their wings,
until care is given and hope is found.

Mosaics decorate the heart
of my mind, disconnected parts
that operate on silent commands
as if spirit alone turns the dial

to a station reminiscent of home,
with silent figures perched
on concrete slabs,
where ears are turned inward and
souls remain in silence. And reasons
come and go without ownership,

denial or guilt to soothe the senses
and point slickened fingers

toward the less guilty and
ignoble of us all in veiled efforts
to control the point-spread,
hasten the outcome.

Excess

They left with their hands outstretched,
ready for another windfall of blood-stained currency
squeezed from the rank and file of the company
that grew out of inflated egos and bottom line subtleties.

"The quicker the rise, the shorter the fall,"
it has been said. And few can argue that the
Fall of Enron came without warning to those
with fat wallets and Hamptons vacation homes.

But slaps on the hand and white-collar jails
do little to feed the jobless and heal the sick
who can no longer afford healthcare and insurance,
let alone house payments and over-due bills.

Without conscience or remorse, what thousands
built a handful collapsed with button-down, three-piece
precision, with little left in the wake of a home for many
and a carpet-bagged, silk-lined coffer to others.

The till was drained before its time
and the slick and the sick got away with
more profit than the losses they gained, written off
in control of lives, past present and future.

For those who gave more than they received
penance is little retribution for retirements lost
and red-inked contracts forgotten like the storms
of winters past and present.

The silkened web still continues to deceive and
weave its dark spell above and beyond what is
recognized or written from the darkened multi-layered
shadows of legalese and constricted contrition.

Ball Point Poet

A lyrical wave of your hand punctuates a life scattered
with the debris of debt and desolation
as T-s are crossed with thumb and forefinger
and I-s are dotted with a fist, held high into the air,
that opens to caress and test line after delicious line
with a voice of passion ripe with experience
and full of the pain that has been the driver,
as relentless as a southwest monsoon,
to where you have always been
in the eyes of destiny and desire.

Peering into the crowd, past, present and future
arrive as one and are immediately transfixed
by the power, absolute and direct, of your presence
and the delicate conviction of a delivery
meant to compel and enable those in attendance
to understand and believe the integrity of the words.

As each admirer comes forward pages are signed
and hands are grasped as hearts are humbled
by your compassion in their presence
on this hot and humid mid-summer's night
and it is realized, once and for all
that you are coming home—once again
as arms, open wide and welcoming, wrap around you
with acceptance and appreciation of choices made
and steps taken to boldly claim a self
caught napping and a soul caught flapping
on the treadmill of a lifetime spent in haste
and a heart full of the waste of unrequited love.

Into the light the Angels have pulled you from afar
whispering your name in honor of the divine spirit
that without prejudice fills the deeper well of inspiration
that enabled you to reach into a past littered with scars
marking the passage of promise of the mission until
ears are pricked to rapt attention and critics are forever silenced.

A Symbiotic Refrain

And what of this muse of my madness,
this all-consuming cacophonic craft of creation
that ceaselessly drives me from comforting arms
toward and over a hauntingly familiar edge
of despair, insecurity, poverty and incisive pain
ever-relentless in its insistent lyrical lure
of release from the ties that torment—and

How much longer will the charade last
as I rhyme my life from within cells of solitude
while continuing to be without its sustenance
and acknowledging the paths of other disparate denizens
who penned past the point of extinction
mythic parables in the direction of deaf ears—where

Home and rest for the soul is unknown...
in a life where the corners have no names
while making a million decisions with little meaning
for my heart is a jagged-edged puzzle
in aimless pursuit of its missing-in-action pieces
as time stills in veiled anticipation—of

Canyons and confusion echoing from the point of no return
urging reply from ne'er-do-well money mongers
with eternity measured in discordant heart-beats
as faceless images advance and retreat without relief
continuing to taunt as the tease is sharpened
urging the final count of ten to be taken—until

Sabotage of self is readily evident...
in an unsolicited effort to understand the persistent pain
when veins are emptied of life's metaphors
testing the waters of the eternal fountain
as it anoints and whets a starving being
hungry for what it contains—and what it all means...

Dances With Wolves

As I stand under an endless sea of blue
alone—in the middle of forever
my longing fingers stretch to the horizon
flexing to touch wavering stalks of gold.
I know without speaking a word
that at last I am home.
In the waning moments of daylight
I will two-step with Two Socks
and touch the Earth with my Heart.
Before the breaking of another dawn
an ocean of buffalo will come and go
in an ancient rite of passage;
their days among us soon to be cut short.
Dances With Wolves I am called;
because my skin of white
bends its knee to the red soul within.
I am lost and found in a vacuum of time;
knowing the future—yet wanting to forget.
There is a time and a place for everything
on this frontier of forever...
as the Tribes of the People pass away
under a sea of rhetorical beliefs
and an ocean of ignorantly spilled blood;
while their ways will follow those of the buffalo.
My brothers will go—and the whites will come;
as one cycle ends and another steadily begins.

Amen

Couples and threes
   procession and prayer
   pastors and passive robed
   figures cloaked
   in good and evil
   precisely parade
   through the congregation
   with hands raised
   and eyes shut...

Exalting that which
   is supposedly higher than them.
   Hopeless attainment
   aspired by many
   gained by a very few;
   with veiled singing
   praising Him—on high.
   Devoid of emotion
   and lacking lustre.

Directed empathic choruses
   lack meaning or understanding.
   It began on cue...
   and with precise fanfare
   ended on cue.
   I went to church
   last night;
   for the last time
   again—amen.

Whispers...

The breath of life
carries us as
winds of change
bend willow trees
almost past the point
and beyond the edge
of what is known
to another place
in another time
of new experiences
and unfamiliar feelings
without restraint
without guilt
without fear—as
the breath of life
carries us... home.

Epitaph for a Poet   (after *Possession* by A.S. Byatt)

And, what would they say...
upon stumbling onto a trove of neglected missives
long forgotten and longer still past their prime
with meanings lost among gathering dust-mites—
whispered and written.. not for me and not for thee?

Would these turners of moss-covered stones
seek to disembowel long-silent thoughts and musings
shuddered and uttered by poets and others
long past and passed over in their literary lifetime
only to rise to fame and fortune in memory and in death?

Ego inflamed and undaunted by the ashes of the remains
questing pinchers disturb hearts napping and owls flapping
as sonnets and soliloquies that were penned in a night
are rudely and discourteously awakened by lust and luck
and were whispered and written, not for me and not for thee.

I ask, "Tread not too harshly on their musty remains"
as seekers and scholars alike are wont to trespass
into the sanctity of the silenced tomb and the tilted stone
persevering to understand what cannot be understood
without the pleasure (or pain) of personal presence.

Ink-stained fingertips impatiently turn encrusted pages
with blinders and bids and indices of many 3x5 hues
at the ready to cautiously categorize and systematically
control secret yearnings and breathless familiarities and
private passions whispered and written.. not for me and not for thee.

House of cards...

Bits and Pieces

Like snowflakes on the tip of a tongue
my childhood fades away in its exposure
to the elements of consistent confusion
from too many moves, too many times
so that there is almost nothing to tell
of times spent with childhood friends
and "Superman" flights of fancy
into uncharted maps of the mind
with little to show for the effort.

Bounced from threshold to threshold
with no lick of the stamp for permanence
of place and peace of a mind
left hanging in the balance of lives
scattered across the heart of California
from heat-soaked, wind-swept walnut groves
to cement and steel 100-degree summer stays;
a hobo in training with little aid of guidance
walked a crooked mile with no end in sight.

Bits and pieces clutter the corridors
of a mind left to care for itself
without counsel or care of its presence
in a life burdened with responsibility;
too much to bear, too much of the time
for a mother with little hope or help
to ford the stream of time as it slipped
through worn and calloused, outstretched fingertips
into an existence of complacency and condemnation.

Why?

Mothers and fathers
and drugs and booze
there is no way to win
you can only lose.

Never knowing when
or who would be home
there is nowhere to turn
when you're always alone.

Constantly running away
from straining hearts and hands
and forever too scared
to stay and take a stand.

In a broken home divided
and devoid of family ties
when there is no love
all that's left—are the lies.

The truth is avoided
and a part of the game
once the mask is donned
you are never the same.

House of Cards

With a foundation of air
and walls of sodden cardboard,
no thicker than the shell of an egg
the house of cards was begun.

Year after year toothpicks were added
to walls and floors as the thickness of the fog
enveloped and swathed the house
in a feigned attempt to cover the pain.

Without a nail and with addresses unknown
the house was moved from town to town
with little to show of the soul for the effort
to claim a slice of life in the living.

Two years here and there,
then five and six to mark the spot
of the degradation of the assembled
left to crawl from the mire.

Guilt and Innocents

No matter how many
words are written or spoken
there can never be
a full understanding of a life lived
with little or no history
to support the fallacies
of misunderstandings
meant to sever the strings
and circumvent the ties
that seemed to bind
what could have never been...
even in continued retrospect
of the untruths and misdeeds
served on innocents,
ignorant of gain or loss,
only knowing of the missing.

Ignorant Desires

Remembrances of sleepwalking into the night
and vaulting over backyard fences served
to remind me over the years of how much
I wanted to leave and be in a place of peace;
a home of love and respect, acceptance and support,
without the constancy of stupor and sluggishness.

Loss of memory can be a simple tool
to enable the forgetting of the negative
and unmentionable moments of a life
lost to unspoken history, not to be shared
with friends or family alike for the fear
of the awakening of the mind.

Ignorant desires can fan flames of neglect
fueled to white-hot spears sharpened
to a pin-point for the tossing of the guilt
into the mire of misbegotten gain
and tarnished rewards, forgotten long ago
in the heat and the heart of the battle.

In the letting go of the shame and the blame
the heart is ready to release the burdened weight
it has held for too many years without solace,
without acknowledgement of the price
for the "pleasure" of the pain.

The Sound of the Bell

Her eyes were empty as she approached,
"Please get a mop and clean the stairs," she said.

Like gladiators in the arena, two men fought
over the possession of a woman,
without thought of love or compassion
only victory over one another;
to the victor goes the spoils!

The knock on the door was urgent
as he went to answer it,
unaware that the one on the other
side would soon undo all
that he thought was his.

As the door opened, one stood back
in surprise as the other moved forward,
into a life of unknown peril and pain
through which there would be no return,
no trophies for the showcase.

The singer was the first to swing,
turning the clerk's head sharply,
as blood began to flow unrestrained
with no end and no saviour in sight
to bless or condemn the action of ego.

It took less than a few minutes
before the bell rang and the towel was thrown,
with one at the bottom of the cement stairs
and the other with a fist waving
as if in seemed victory the prize was his.
It was over before it started
as the one with the sarcastic smile
was never to return to the side
of the mother who never could be
the apple in any man's eye.

Sisters

All, ladies in waiting, as you each bided time
held in breathless anticipation
of the moment of release to the arms
of saviors impatient in the waiting.

From the illusion of a painted house
seeds were planted to be watered ...
sown at times demanded by decree
of individual necessity and intended release.

If the end was supposed to satisfy the means
a few were misguided in their quests
of discovery, security, and solace
on paths of matrimony and partnership.

Incomplete lives shared by all
within or without walls of plenty
while the weakness of the bonds
were subtly evident to the multitude.

Lives lived in feigned satisfaction
built on foundations of myth
drew the paths followed in silence
with little left to the fulfillment.

As it is "dust to dust and ashes to ashes,"
each was followed by the other to the end
of lives led in acquiescence and recompense
with little left but the legacies of the lost.

To The Accounting

In a direction unknown
the faucet flows
and water spills
into the streets:
Lyon, Bosworth, Circular,
Inverness Drive,
Sonoma Mountain Road;
and too many cities of
no consequence, no matter.

The drought continues
as nourishment rescinds itself
without deliberation, and arid
blood-beds lay in wait,
as if divine intervention
is lending a hand, and
lifeless souls bake in the sun
with hearts exposed
to scorching rays.

To behold the truth, the
cunning of the living,
and the uneven remains of
the dead: hollow voices
filling no voids, adding
nothing, invisible ink,
the is nothing to do
and no one to turn to
when it comes to the accounting.

Between You and Me

In the conversation we never had,
I ask you about my childhood
and of memories lost and found
in the passage of a life forever mending.

You tell me about your love for us,
the children of your heart's desire
cast into a place of discontent and confusion
on the way to your self… never found.

I want to ask about the choices of need
made without thought of self or soul,
effortless moments of collective good
within the fog of support and solace.

Across the table a drag is taken
on the instrument of your departure
in addition to the addictions you sought
to camouflage a multitude of supposed sins.

Forgiveness is a word bantied about
in feigned attempts at resolution
before the passing of the night calls a name
but not a memory that seeks to linger.

My heart never forgets all you gave
to the three you would call your own;
perhaps only those would receive
the love you held so close.

In the conversation we never had
I tell you I understand how choices made
were borne of the need to support
three to the draw without a pair to the hold.

The Crossing

Slow moving lava lamp,
liquid dreams of
my days and nights
for nine months (more or less).
I couldn't take it anymore...
and the crossing,
Like Jonah crawling
from the darkest depths
of the whale,
came just after dawn
peeled its blurred eyes
and my mother had spent another night
two-stepping and four-count waltzing
in the taverns and bars
of Market Street.

Fleshy, dimpled legs
spread and stirrups ready,
one hand, then two
yanked me, in the waking hours
of a new day, to a world
not of my choosing,
not of my desire;
perhaps even, not
of my time.

Tugged and wrenched
into breath, arms flailed
and battleship lungs
bombarded the room
with blasts of anger and
volleys of frustration,
as scars, proud flesh already
preparing to cover the truth
of the lies told before birth,
decorated my body and

readied my heart and soul
for what was to come.

Louder than the wail
of a new-born calf,
a virgin heart bursting
and blood pulsing
through satin thin veins,
arrival announced
and the beginning
of my march on life
and my assault toward
discovery began.

Shadow Self

Hidden pain is a luxury
I can no longer afford.
Already, it has been too long
in the revealing, the exposing,
the surrendering of spirit,
the release of emotion,
the telling, the crying,
the crying, the crying.

More than fifty years
of solitude…
within a shadow of blame,
a construct of shame—with
nowhere to turn when
cloaked in a shroud
of remorse and guilt
for the doing of nothing. The
doing of nothing.

Without a net, sustenance,
sustenance of spirit, something
to hold onto, tombstones called
a name unknown, reflective
of a family divided from
each other and self,
with hands held behind backs
and slippery fingers crossed.

The same tune played over,
and over, and over,
until none would listen,
none would respond
to the cry of the wolf,
the wail of anonymnity,
the words too much spoken
to ears no longer open, to
ears no longer open.

Fool's Gold

Naked... she stood
at the foot of her mother-bed,
a big, feather-stuffed womb
for a boy's body that faked a fever
and was no match
for the flames of burning skin.

An eight year-old son
with little else on his mind
but idolizing thoughts of...
Lash LaRue, Hopalong Cassidy,
Roy Rogers and Trigger,
felt the surge of lust
and the agony of first response
when the cotton spread
began to rise, and
between hairless legs
his penis, taught and rigid
with a mind of its own,
summoned the strength
for an adolescent journey
yet to be understood.

As her slip fell onto
the floor, in a careless pile
with the rest of the
discarded clothing—and
she pulled the covers back,
careful to not get too close
to what he was becoming,
or who he wanted to be,
and what he had no idea of
what he wanted to do
on that most wonderful,
"everything will be fine" day.

The First Cut

I have cut a new eye,
a new vein of perception
to see the seed of my life,
to feel the opening of the flower,
the peeling of the sour grape;
veins flowing & exposed.

More than half the way
to the shores of Galilea,
I have turned for
one more look,
one more peek;
a last quest
for understanding;
for knowledge of
what lay under the mask
never finished.

A mad mother in hand
with a liquid drunk to
guide the way of
three stones, unturned,
connected at birth
and in need of sustenance,
six tiny hands to man
the oars; to ply the seas.
I have cut a new eye,
to slice through the ambiguity,
in the shadow of my death—and
the supposed blame of my birth.

Follow the Leader

With no leaders for the battles or guides for the trails
my direction was faulted at best as I scanned the horizon
for signs of familiar life among the littered waste of broken
promises offered with fingers too-long crossed for the lying.

Few were there as I looked for parental meaning
in the midnight meanderings and twilight offerings
of the many who were blinded by the light of imagined safety
and the benefit of a barbed wire existence in support of self.

"Fathers" without name or presence came and went...
in and out of a life too young for the grasping of the meaning
of a search for support from the few who dared to offer a life
for the trade of a soul left wanting for completion.

As the tides of indifference were swept into existence
there was little recompense for the two-year lives
left in the dust for the sweeping under the rug
and the covering of the conscience, too weak for the truth.

Remission

Upstairs, on the second floor
of the tract home, more than 200 rectangular
two-story plans with little variance, I retreated...
away from the noise, the shouting,
the degrading, the accusations, the shouting.

A quiet haven, behind the door, in the eave
of the house on 451 Inverness Street, where
no one could find me in my place of hiding,
my place of solace, my place... my place.

Barely standing up I could listen,
but I could not hear, did not want to hear
drunken fits of rage, pointing fingers, nothing of sense,
nothing of value, pounding into my brain, seeping
into places of little recovery, little solace.

An elementary school existence of fear,
of apprehension that left me numb of feeling
and with none but a fleeting memory
of time spent in seclusion in a triangle
of surplus emotions and duplicitous pledges.

None the better for neighbors trenched in ruts
of lives in waiting, lives in remission,
lives in lies and shadows of truth,
each in the corners of fault and revulsion,
on their way to an ending of no consequence.

A sound-proofed heart searched for direction;
pleaded for absolution, without response
to his wanting, to his desire, to his desire...
as few knew of the thin-edged existence
on the second floor, in rectangular retreat.

All are the same. All are different. All are absent.

Silent Vigil

With her death
my mother took
my childhood, imprisoned
as it was in the darkest
depths of my invisible self.

Lest I be judged,
placed in position,
recognized,
the dark self consumed
the light,
the brightest wick
of my childhood;
to melt years into
puddles of wax,
thin drippings
of solitude to eliminate
the fear of knowing;
the anxiety of memory,
the dull bite
of abrasive pain.

With her death,
my youth remains
in question,
languishing
without clarity;
a soliloquy
without substance.

Mountaintops and Memories

Mostly at a loss as to
what to do when asked by
others to come and play.
Backyard construction zones;
earthmovers of tin and steel,
rubber tires rolling,
dust and dirt flying and piling
higher and higher.

In turn, I was afraid to ask, afraid
they would come…
they would come and see
the you that was not me,
that was not you as
you could not be.

Liquid or powder, it made
little difference to your thirst,
the hunger for haze…
among the crazed indifference
of relationships squandered;
family dispersed in the distance.

Mountaintops and memories
of sleep-induced stupors
feigning normalcy; out of
sight and mind, out of
body, out of time…
out of the time we never had.

Choice No Choice

Count 'em!
One hazy year
after the other,
after the other;
childhood memories
and formative years,
stolen
at the swallow
of a pill:
one, two, three…
by a mother
with little strength
to fight black-cloaked demons,
attacking
and burrowing into
a defenseless soul.

Slick, oval instruments
of silkened silence
masking the sting
of regret
and supposed failure
in the eyes of God
and family alike.

Haunted by unrelenting
ghost of children
whose misguided lives
drove feigned choices,
blind woman lashing out
at the nothingness,
you lived your life
in fear,
lived you life
without love,
lived your life
with the emptiness
of a mother who lost

a child at birth.

Unbearable pain
(imagined or other)
brought
speedy & sneaky
midnight deliveries,
fueled by fake,
shaky approvals,
and like the fall
of a bird with wings
of melting wax,
the darkness
of the deepening abyss
claimed you...
again and again and again.

After too many times
for too many years
you became a blur
in my loving eyes
(Rita Hayworth no more);
hell or heaven on earth,
it was all the same
to you;
no matter, no mother.

Do You Hear What I Hear?

Voices crying in the night;
shouting at the dark,
crouching in the shadows,
bats circling tombstones,
afraid of the touch,
reeling from the pain
of abstinence and neglect.

Like being the loser
in a fifteen-round
free-for-all match,
my ears echo the stupor
of a mother and father
spewing drunken venom,
providing a certain source
of ironic entertainment
during the years when he
should have been teaching
me how to drive and she
about love, not hate;
about respect, not apathy;
about life, not death;
about compassion, not anger.

No matter where I turn,
shame lingers, tucked into
dark, uncertain corners,
shadowy and insistent,
and netherworld voices
taunt me with vapid promises
of inclusion to a family dispersed,
without ties, without duty.

Do you hear what I hear…

The Memory of Fog

I picked my way through the fog,
white line by white line,
seeing no farther than the end
of the car, a remembrance of
a childhood spent in dreams
and fantasy.

It covers the cuts and shields
the wounds of the mindless
forgetfulness and the searing
of the knife-sharpened tongues,
honed to a perfect edge by
years of practice and performance.

Enveloped by its thickness, a
seeming protection, a blanket
of safety from the fear of the fight,
the fear of the cry, the fear of
the hunger, the fear...
of the drowning fear.

In a tomb of my own making,
a casket of wood and lathe I hid;
far from the pain and the
reckoning and the suffering,
farther still from the memory
of loss and love.

Fog can erase the memory;
cease time to exist, and
cover dormant fault lines
with a blanket as dense as that
of a wall that serves to divide

a soul in the wanting.

Falling darkness, gathering mist &
fading memories all become one &
all become the same in the fog,
in the fog, in the fog.

Ignorant Desires

Remembrances of sleepwalking into the night
and vaulting over backyard fences served
to remind me over the years of how much
I wanted to leave and be in a place of peace;
a home of love and respect, acceptance and support,
without the constancy of stupor and sluggishness.

Loss of memory can be a simple tool
to enable the forgetting of the negative
and unmentionable moments of a life
lost to unspoken history, not to be shared
with friends or family alike for the fear
of the awakening of the mind.

Ignorant desires can fan flames of neglect
fueled to white-hot spears sharpened
to a pin-point for the tossing of the guilt
into the mire of misbegotten gain
and tarnished rewards, forgotten long ago
in the heat and the heart of the battle.

In the letting go of the shame and the blame
the heart is ready to release the burdened weight
it has held for too many years without solace,
without acknowledgement of the price
for the "pleasure" of the pain.

Another Close Call

Smoky death mask,
creeping under
bedroom door,
its graying tentacles
stretched
full and strong,
skeletal knuckles exposed,
grasping & pulling
without conscience.
A killer,
pure of mission,
pure of deed
answered
your ignorant call,
mother,
and taunted me
even in fitful sleep.

Alarms stun senses
struggling to awaken,
fumbling open
the door to a
sightless hallway
offering no response
to the cries and the callings
amid hazy figurines
dancing—to an evil
and eerie ghost dance
cadence.

Three rooms away,
drugged and asleep,
seemingly unaware
of the tightening noose
creeping near,
steadily closing
to embezzle last breath,
quicksand pulls you

deeper with each wave—of
surrender,
you fought no more,
you fought no more.

Surrounding stench
engulfed
a trembling boy
rushing to face
arms burned
to pooling vinyl;
scalding
white-hot flames
inhaling my breath
as I kitchen-knifed
charcoal encrusted skin
to hour-glass freedom,
slipping away with
each drugged step.

The butt of a Parliament cigarette,
its filter still smoking,
stuck to bony,
fire-red fingers
as I dragged you
from the intended tomb;
a limp body cradled
in the arms of a son,
grasped for life,
no more;
fought for love,
no more;
surviving another close call,
another toss of the boxcars.

The Silence of Dreams

I can dream of you in the silence of the night
and think of how I see you now
with a warm heart and all the tenderness
you wanted but could never give.

A wounded angel left alone in a land
of temptation and ruin with strength
auctioned off at the lowest bid
and the drop of the executioner's bloody hand.

You beckon for silence as I follow breathlessly
into the meadow of your motherhood
bright with wildly blooming flowers
and succulent scents billowing on the wind.

But too soon the wilt begins and the sourness
invades a misguided wish of a life
that never could have been without
the lure of the toxins that claimed your soul.

They crawled at your feet and tugged
at your heart without mercy
as you fought with claws and cries
until you were no more... a shell.

I can dream of you in the silence of the night
and think of how I see you now
with Parliaments and coffee to brighten a day
and a time too soon in the ending.

for Annie...

CPSIA information can be obtained at www.ICGtesting.com

261075BV00004B/2/P

9 780983 349822